Joe Got Flow

Chris E. James

ISBN: 1727128354
ISBN-13: 978-1727128352

Illustration by Leron McAdoo aka Ron Mc of Backyard

DEDICATION

This book is dedicated to all the young writers I have worked with over the years and the ones to come. I appreciate you all being so willing to express your thoughts, ideas, feeling and opinions through poems. Your bravery to be open and honest impacts the world way more than you probably realize. For that, I thank you.

To every organization that has worked behind the scenes to assure my presence in a classroom, I appreciate you; Arkansas Learning through the Arts, Arkansas A+, Wildwood Park for the Arts, Thea Foundation and Arkansas Arts Council.

This book is dedicated to my favorite young poets, Tashia Mayo, Jamee and Norel McAdoo. You three make me want to sharpen my writing skills. Keep challenging us old heads to keep writing.

Thank you to everyone who encouraged me to write poetry. It all started when I was a kid. I saw a stack poems in my brother, Rod's closet. He made me to want to write and I did. My 7th grade science teacher, Ms. Pilar Murphy always encouraged me to keep writing. She used to hype me up and make me believe I could actually go somewhere as a writer. In the 11th grade, my english teacher Mrs. Jones at North Little Rock sparked the fire once again. She pushed me to keep writing.

Thank you Stacey James McAdoo for editing this book and congrats to you for being recognized as Regional Arkansas Teacher of the Year. Thank you Ron Mc of BackYard enterprises for being a dope illustrator.

Thank you to my amazing mother for holding on to my very first poetry notebooks from almost 20 years ago. Thank you.

Lastly, this book is dedicated to the love of my life. Her name is poetry. Thank you.

CONTENTS

ACKNOWLEDGMENTS

Yo! Yo! Yo! Welcome to the beginning of the book. I hope this book is truly an experience for you. I don't want you to only read this book. I need you to participate in all the activities. At the end of each chapter, there is an exercise. Do it. Doing these exercises will ensure that you are comprehending the information. Lets go poet!

Chapter 1
Joe Got A Dream

Every kid has a dream. Some kids dream of being a doctor or a zoologist. Some kids dream of being a fireman or police officer. Others dream of being the next Lebron James or Steph Curry. But Joseph was like no other. He dreamed of being just like his older brother. He wanted to be a rapper, wear expensive clothes and be dapper. He dreamed of bright lights and big stages. He dreamed of sharing his braggadocious lyrics from notebook pages. Every day he would stand in front of the bathroom mirror pretending to be famous.

Even when he was wide awake he was dreaming.

It was his 5th grade school year and the month was October. He was excited because the school talent show was getting closer. November 13th was the big day. He counted down the days, the hours, the minutes and even the seconds. This would be the year he'd become a star.

At home he would try on different outfits, shoes and hats as if he was preparing for a fashion show. He would practice all the latest dance moves until he was tired and sweating. He would practice all his lyrics so he wouldn't forget 'em. He was dedicated. He knew in order to be the best he had to work harder than the rest. So he did exactly that. While his friends were playing video games and watching all the latest YouTubers, he was learning new ways to be better in the future.

Monday morning his dad woke him up for school. "Wake up Joseph. Get out the bed." Joseph woke up excited as he always did. Ready to learn something new, he washed his face and brushed his teeth. He ran out the house, in a rush, so he wouldn't miss the bus. Joseph wrote new rhymes the entire ride. When he finally made it to school, he went straight to class. Joseph skipped breakfast to work more on his craft.

"Good morning Ms. Morning," Joseph spoke to his teacher as he walked in class. Ms. Morning asked, "What are you in a hurry to work on today?" Joseph replied, "A rap song for the talent show." Ms. Morning asked if she could hear what he had so far. Joseph replied, "Sure. Can you kick me a beat?" Ms. Morning laughed and then agreed. She grabbed a pencil and started tapping on the table and beat boxing like she was Doug E Fresh. Joseph stood up and started giving his all.

"I'm the best at what I do because I won't stop. I'm 10 years old and I'm the prince of Hip Hop. Something like Bow Wow but I got more style. The girls on the playground say they like my smile. I make A's and B's for the honor roll so when I get older I can buy diamonds and gold. Bars!" Ms. Morning put down the pencil out of breath from beatboxing. She yelled with excitement as she hugged Joseph. "Oh my God! Joseph that was so good." Ms. Mornings' compliments made Joseph blush uncontrollably. Then Ms. Morning went on to ask Joseph how he learned to use couplets so well.

Joseph looked at Ms. Morning with confusion. "What's a couplet," Joseph asked. "Really, Joseph? It's what you're using in your raps," Ms. Morning explained. She went on to explain that a couplet is two lines where the end words rhyme. "For example, you said, I'm the best at what I do because I won't stop. I'm 10 years old and I'm the prince of Hip Hop," Ms. Morning explained further, "You had two complete sentences and the last word in your first sentence rhymed with the last word in the second sentence. Together those two sentences (or lines) make a couplet." She went to the whiteboard and wrote down more examples of couplets.

I found love.

It was in the heavens above.

The wind is blowing.

It may be snowing.

I jumped in the cold river.

It made me shiver.

I always remember.

The month was November.

You have a nice car.

Do you drive it far?

"Joseph, couplets are used in most of the songs you hear every day. Listen to rappers like Tupac, Nas, J. Cole, Future or even singers like Chris Brown, Beyonce, Cardi B and you'll hear couplets. But the type of writers that use couplets the most are poets. Poets like Maya

Angelou, Langston Hughes, Nikki Giovanni, Phyllis Wheatley, Saul Williams, Tashia Mayo, Stacey McAdoo, Marquese McFergson and the list goes on. And oh my God! I almost forgot. One of my favorite poets, Chris James. He is actually coming to the classroom to teach all the 5th graders about poetry and figurative language next week. Joseph you're going to love him. In the meantime keep writing those couplets."

For the rest of the week Joseph wrote couplets in his rap notebook. He was excited to learn that he had been using this style of writing so naturally and didn't even know it. When Joseph got home he listened to songs and wrote down all the rhyming words he heard trying to discover the couplets. He was indeed on the way to becoming a poet and didn't know it.

Exercise #1- Listen to songs and discover the rhyming words/ the couplets and then write your own.

Chapter 2
The Bearded Poet

The next Monday rolled around. Joseph got off the bus and hurried straight to class as he always did. He walked in to notice Ms. Morning wasn't alone. She instead sat on top of her desk laughing and going on with an unfamiliar man with a big black beard. Ms. Morning noticed Joseph and quickly summoned him over to meet her guest. "Joseph, this is Chris James, the poet I told you who would visit our classroom this week. Mr. Chris, this is Joseph, the young rapper I was just telling you about." Joseph confidently reached up to shake Mr. Chris' hand. "Nice to meet you sir." Mr. Chris smiled, then gripped Joseph's hand and pulled him for a hug as he stated, "This is how brothers show love." Joseph looked at him and replied, "Okaaaaaaayyyy." Mr. Chris laughed and said to Joseph, "I'm excited to hear your poems this week." Joseph responded, "I don't write poems. I am a rapper." Mr. Chris looked at Joseph with an intense stare and said, "Where in the world do you think rap comes from little man? It derives from poetry." "How is that Mr. Chris," Joseph asked. "By the end of this week you'll know exactly what I mean young Joseph. I will show you that in order to be a dope rapper you must first master the skills of a great poet."

The bell rang and all the students came running in. Once everyone was settled, Ms. Morning instructed everyone to take out a notebook and pencil. She then informed them that for today and the rest of the week a special guest would be in the classroom teaching everyone some really awesome writing skills. "Class, we have the honor of having a national award- winning poet and playwright by the name of Chris James in our school all week long.

So everyone listen up, show respect and give Mr. Chris a big warm welcome." Everyone roared and clapped loudly.

3

Mr. Chris ran up to the front of the class and screamed, "Yo Yo Yo! Thanks for having me young poets. We are going to start out with a song. I'm going to sing the line first and then you all repeat after me. Alright, here we go."

Mr. Chris began with, "Woke up this morning, poetry on my mind..."
The kids repeated it back but sounded like nobody's choir because absolutely no one was in sync. "Whoa. Whoa. Whoa. Let's pause that and try it again. That sounded like some hurt whales," Mr. Chris jokingly stated to the class. Everyone laughed at Mr. Chris' unapologetic truth. Then they tried again.

Woke up this morning, poetry on my mind.
Words from my soul on these notebook lines.
No money for food, no money for gas.
All I got is my pen and my pad.

"Give it up for yourselves. That was pretty good," Mr. Chris said with a smile of approval. "Alright let's do it. This week I will be facilitating you all in writing some of the best poems ever. First, I need you to know that poetry is art. So get ready because this week we are painting." The kids jumped and yelled in excitement. Mr. Chris then said, "Unfortunately, we don't have any canvases so we will use paper instead. And since we don't have any paint brushes we will use pencils. Aw man! We don't have any paint either so we will use our words. Yes, we are painting pictures with our words."

Everyone looked at Mr. Chris with confusion. "What I am saying is, I want you to write with so much detail and description that I can see exactly what's happening in your story or poem. I'll start by sharing one of my poems." Mr. James stretched his arms and lowered his head and jumped up and down like he was preparing to play in a basketball game. He slowly lifted up his head and began sharing his poem.

Life Is...... By Chris James

Life ain't always what it seems.

Somedays it's like a dream.

Fairytales maybe

Butterflies and bees

Birds looking down on everyone from their trees.

Other days the skies are dark

Spooky sounds from all angles while you walk

through the park.

Nightmares sometimes haunt you while you sleep.

The scariest thoughts find their way into your

mind and creep.

When it thunders

it rains.

Last night I made music while staring through the

window pane.

What's wrong with pain?

Is it something to gain?

Why some things and people stay the same?

Maybe they're afraid of change.

Life ain't no game but be careful how you play.

The cards you're dealt

Can determine your life's outcome.

Be cool, slow down, don't run

Life ain't always what it seems but it is exactly

always and forever what you make it.

Mr. Chris stepped back and took a bow. The kids clapped in amazement at how Mr. Chris used his words and performed with so much expression, passion and volume in his voice. "Thank you so much for listening. So if you will, raise your hand and tell me what rhyming words you heard and what images or things could you imagine as I recited my poem." Everyone's hand went up quickly. They were ready to give their answer. Mr. Chris scanned the room slowly. He walked in a circle around the room while singing, "Eeny, meeny, miny, moe. Catch a tiger by its toe…" As he finished the old school nursery rhyme he turned and pointed at Joseph.

Joseph stood up with his rap notebook in hand and shared aloud every single rhyming word Mr. Chris had just recited. Mr. Chris looked at him and said, "Kid you're something special." Joseph looked at Mr. Chris and said, "Nah. I'm just a rapper. I kinda know this stuff." Mr. Chris smiled and nodded as he replied, "Okay young rapper poet, I hear you. Alright now everyone else, tell me what images you saw."

After about five minutes of breaking down the images in Mr. Chris' poem, he then instructed everyone to write their own poem. "The focus question for today's writing is 'What is my dream world?' Be sure to write with detail. Paint pictures with your words. You have 10 minutes. Tomorrow, be ready to share these poems aloud."

Everyone grabbed their paper and pencil and began writing their masterpieces. Joseph leaned back in his chair and thought to himself how easy this task would be. In just 5 minutes he was already done. Joseph was talented but he was hard headed. He thought he had nothing more to learn. He'd soon discover that was untrue.

Exercise # 2 Before you go to the next chapter, I want you to write a poem too. Paint pictures with your words. What is your dream world?

Chapter 3
More to Learn

It was Tuesday morning. All the students sat at their desks looking over the poems they wrote the day before. Mr. Chris walked in with his beard shining, teeth showing and bowtie fresh to death. "Yo yo yo! What's up class? Who is ready to share these amazing poems," Mr. Chris asked with excitement. The majority of the class raised their hands - eager to go first. "I love volunteers. We will just go by tables. Let's start with the table in the back," Mr. Chris instructed. The students began reading their poems.

Joshua Edwards
10/16/17
Ms. Morning's 5th Grade

My World Poem

In my world no one has to die to go to heaven.

We already live there.

It's here.

Everywhere you are happy

is heaven.

Heaven is your place of peace.

Peace is in your mind.

Peace is a state of mind.

Peace is your heaven.

Home is my peace.

My mother is the queen of all angels.
Instead of hats

She wears a halo.

I watch her glow at night.

When the room is dark

she remains the light.

She got that God glow.

Keep sinking things afloat.

She got that God flow.

She is the river and the boat.

My world is heaven and my dad is the angel at
the gate.

He also makes sure the grass and clouds are
mowed.

And me, I get to be a kid forever and play video
games with Martin Luther King, Prince, Michael
Jackson, Muhammad Ali, Aliyah, Left Eye, Whitney
Houston.

This is my dream world.

Brittany Hamilton

10/16/17

Ms. Morning's 5th Grade

A Pink World

My car, my house, my dog, my clothes, my cell
phone are all pink.

In my world, girls rule.
Only boys have to follow the rules.
Michelle Obama and Oprah are Co-Presidents of the
United States of America.
Beyonce and Rihanna are over Congress.
My favorite Aunt Leslie is the leader of the FBI.
In my world, dreams come true.
People accept you for being you.
No one has to change to be cool.
In my world, girls eliminate all bullying in every
school.
In my world, girls are powerful and comfortable
in their skin.
Girls play sports against boys and always win.
In my world, hate is no more and love is the
beginning and the end.

Everyone shared their poems. Mr. Chris expressed that
he was quite impressed. Some students read loud and
with a lot of expression. Others were quiet and couldn't
get over their shyness. But Mr. Chris explained to them
that it was okay because many students were sharing
aloud for the first time. Mr. Chris was most satisfied that

they even shared at all. But it wasn't over. He saved the best for last. He and Ms. Morning both knew that Joseph would be among the most interesting in the class. Mr. Chris put on his radio voice, "Alright, everybody. It ain't over yet. We saved the best for last. Give it up. Give it up for Joe the Rapper."

Joseph stood up like he was 6 feet tall. He had on his Jordan shoes and t-shirt with his favorite rap group on it, The Migos. Joseph picked up his paper. Instead of standing at his desk like all his classmates, he walked to the front of the room. "Alright! Here we go guys. In my world, money is made of trees. Every single one belongs to me. I'm as famous as Usher. I keep the ladies blushin'. I'm MC Hammer and no rapper can touch me. I got a big house and my neighbors all love me. My moms ain't gotta work 'cause I got all the money. Ain't no such thing as winter cause every day is sunny." Joseph ended his rap with a dab and took a bow as if he had just performed the best rap ever.

Mr. Chris stepped to the front of the class and clapped in a very slow motion and grinned at Joseph. Mr. Chris looked at Joseph, placed his hand on his shoulder and said, "Kid you're really talented but I really would like you to at least attempt to write a poem. I guarantee your rap lyrics would be so much better." Joseph replied, "Yeah, but I'm a rapper."

Mr. Chris shook his head with disappointment and said, "Joseph, you should really do some research into where Hip Hop derived from. In the 1970s when Hip Hop was birthed in the Bronx, New York City, it started with the DJ who played the music at the parties and the poet who shared lyrics over the DJ's instrumentals. The poet later became known as the emcee and now a rapper. Joseph, you can't be a rapper without also being a poet."

Joseph looked at Mr. Chris with a blank stare and his shoulders slumped as he responded, "Okay. I'll try it. I'll learn this poetry stuff." Mr. Chris smiled and shook his head up and down as he turned to the class and announced, "Today is going to be a great day. I am so excited to challenge you all to take your writing to the next level. How can we do that you ask? I'll show you. We are going to begin learning a new language, FIGURATIVE LANGUAGE. Write these things down, please. Similes, metaphors, alliteration, personification, idioms, adages and lastly, onomatopoeia." Mr. Chris wrote all of this on the whiteboard.

"Today, we are going to master similes. Similes help you to better paint pictures with your words," Mr. Chris shared. "A simile is a sentence that compares two unlike things using the words LIKE or AS." Mr. Chris wrote several examples on the board.

Simile

The ball is round like an eyeball.

Her hair is curly like a fry.

Usain Bolt is as fast as lightning.

Love is as crazy as a circus.

Joseph has a brain like a computer.

Outside, it is as cold as an icebox.

Ms. Morning is as cool as Antarctica.

"Right now, I need you to write down these examples. Then underline the two things being compared in each sentence. Afterwards identify if the word LIKE or AS is used. If in fact two things are being compared and the word LIKE or AS is used, the sentence is a simile," Mr. Chris informed the class. For the next 3 minutes the students were absolutely silent as they focused on understanding this new thing Mr. Chris was introducing to them.

Mr. Chris walked around peaking over everyone's shoulder to see who was able to identify the reasons these sentences were similes. After making sure everyone understood, he instructed the class to begin writing their own similes for they would soon have to use them in their own writing.

"Alright. Alright. This is a pretty smart class. I'm giving you five minutes to write down as many similes as you can think of. Remember, you are comparing two unlike things using the word LIKE or AS in the sentence. And it has to make sense. Your goal in a simile is to let us know how one thing reminds you of the other," Mr. Chris said to the class.

Student Similes

My room is messy _like_ a pigsty.

Dreams are _like_ movies.

Books are _like_ adventures.

Dogs are as loyal as best friends.
Oranges are as round as a basketball.
The paper was as white as a blanket of snow.

Before the allotted time was up, the students were already asking Mr. Chris to come look at their similes. They were so excited to share their brilliance. Mr. Chris was just as excited. He was excited that they got it, that they were understanding figurative language. Mr. Chris threw his hands in the air and shouted, "Time is up poets. Put down your pencils and prepare to share aloud." Like earlier that day and the day before, many of the students jumped up ready to volunteer to share first. For the next ten minutes of class Mr. Chris sat back and listened to all their well thought out examples.

After they were done sharing aloud, Mr. Chris complimented the class. "Yoooooooo! I can't even front. This is one of the dopest classes I've visited in a while. Y'all are really good. But now that I see you guys get it, lets now use the rest of the class time to write poems using similes." All the students, especially Joseph, sat up with their shoulders straight and eyes on Mr. Chris ready to accept his challenge.

"Okay, here goes. Today, you may choose any of the following topics. You can write about family, friendships, love, school, bullying, war, community, nature, encouragement, life, struggle, poverty, world hunger, segregation, equality or change. That's a lot to choose from. So choose wisely. You have 10 minutes to write. GO!" Mr. Chris started the timer on his phone while Ms. Morning put on some soft Jazz music in the background.

All the students put pencil to paper and began writing. Mr. Chris and Ms. Morning walked around the class to make sure everyone stayed on task. "I see some people thinking too much and writing too little. Focus on writing and not so much about being right," Mr. Chris yelled to encourage those not being as productive. Joseph sat in his seat but he seemed to be more focused than usual. It was obvious that he was genuinely giving this poetry stuff a real try.

After five minutes had passed, Joseph raised his hand to get Mr. Chris' attention. "Hey Mr. Chris! What you think about this so far," Joseph asked. Mr. Chris picked up the paper and read it for a few seconds. Then he looked at Joseph and replied, "Man, you're doing a really good job. Keep it up. You have three more minutes." Joseph grinned as he hurried to continue writing more. He was determined to impress Mr. Chris by proving that he could be a poet and a rapper. Joseph thought to himself *I'ma really be the best at the talent show now.*

The stopwatch on Mr. Chris' phone went off loudly. The students kept writing, unbothered by the alarm. "That means time is up. Put a cherry on the top and wrap it up. In other words, put down the pencils now," Mr. Chris shouted. Actually, he was always shouting. I guess it was his way of keeping the class awake. "Sarah you should go first," Mr. Chris said. Sarah, who is usually the most quiet girl in the class stood up slowly but with confidence and recited;

Sarah Mixon

10/17/17

Ms. Morning's 5th Grade

Sarah Simile Poem

The Earth is a like a house and we all live in it.

We ought to keep it clean.

Imagine your backyard was your bedroom

your neighborhood your kitchen.

Would you still litter?

The ground is not a trash can.

Doesn't deserve to be dirtied up like a dump

yard.

We should keep it pretty.

Be thankful for the trees.

They are the reasons we breathe.

I appreciate the breeze

And I love the leaves.

The flowers are like art.

The ground is a like a grocery store.

It feeds us all that we need.

The rain and the sun work together like business

partners

to ensure the growth of every seed.
Oh how I love the Earth because she loves me like
a mother loves her child.

Everyone was so shocked that Sarah had read her poem with so much expression. This was a new discovery for the class and maybe even for Sarah. Poetry seemed to give her a newfound confidence. For the next twenty minutes Mr. Chris hurried through the students so everyone could share.

Malik Mayo

10/17/17

Ms. Morning's 5th Grade

Malki Simile Poem

The other day I saw a man
balled up like an abandoned dog.
He was cold.
His eyes looked like pain.
His hands and feet were as dark as the ground he
lied on.
He smelt like old sweat and dirty laundry.

He was as thin as a stick.

He was starving.

I wanted to help.

But like most people I kept walking.

He watched people pass him up as they continued talking.

I wish I could silence the world so they could hear his cries.

I wonder if we would stop then.

What if he was your king?

Would you reach out your hand?

Would you take a stand?

Everyone's poem was great and full of substance. Again, Mr. Chris was pleased. Joseph sat in his seat still writing instead of stopping like Mr. Chris had commanded earlier. "Joseph, I know this better be the best poem ever written since you're taking extra time to write. Get up and share it. It's your turn," Mr. Chris said. Joseph stood up, went to the front of the class and shared.

"Here goes. I think it's pretty good by the way," Joseph gloated with confidence.

Joseph Hardaway

10/17/17

Ms. Morning's 5th Grade

The Powerful Nine

1957, in Little Rock, Arkansas
nine brave black kids integrated a school of white
students.
They were treated like trash.
Kicked around like soccer balls.
Still they stood tall.
Even when their backs were against the wall.
They just wanted an equal education.
Treated unfairly because of segregation.
Black skin was treated like a target.
Their bullies aimed to kill.
But they would not allow their dreams to die.
The Little Rock Nine continued to fly
like birds in the sky.
Like me they were determined

and would not stop.
Sometimes great change comes with pain.
Their victory perfectly explains.
Because of their will to fight
I don't have to.
I am as free as a kite.
I can learn just as much as any other race.
I now have the education to compete in the race
and win.
I will win. I will win.

Joseph put down his paper and looked at the class. Ms. Morning looked at Mr. Chris. Mr. Chris looked at Ms. Morning. They both smiled and with the rest the class, they clapped immensely. Mr. Chris walked over to Joseph and said, "Joe you almost got flow now kid. That was really good." Joseph blushed and replied, "Almost got flow?" Mr. Chris shook his head and grinned, "Joe you getting better but it's much more to learn."

Exercise #3- Go write a poem and use at least five similes.

Chapter 4
A Metaphor Type of Day

Day three had arrived. Mr. Chris came to the school early. He walked through the hallway as the students all greeted him with their various greetings.

"What's up Mr. Poet,"... "Mr. Chris you coming to our class today,"... "Mr. Chris, I wrote poem at home,"... "Mr. Chris, can I get a hug,"... "Mr. Chris, you look like James Harden,"... "Mr. Chris, I saw you on YouTube,"... "Mr. Chris, my Mama follow you on Instagram."

The amount of love these students had grown for Mr. Chris in such a short time was heart wrenching. Out of nowhere, Joseph ran up and began walking with Mr. Chris as if they were the best of buddies. "What we doing today?" Joseph asked. Mr. Chris shook Josephs' hand and replied, "Dang! Hello to you, too, Joe the Rapper Poet." Joseph realized it was rude to not speak first before asking questions.

"My bad bearded poet. Great morning to you. Now what are we doing today?" Joseph asked again but with even more enthusiasm. "Man you gon' have to wait and see. Class starts in just five minutes," Mr. Chris said teasing Joseph's young curiosity.

The bell rang and everyone came running into the classroom. The students threw their backpacks on the hook and hurried to hug Mr. Chris while he screamed, "The germs are killing me!

Someone help please!" The students laughed and kept hugging him. "If you can hear me clap once. If you can hear me clap twice," Ms. Morning yelled attempting to calm the students. "Everyone take a seat please so Mr.

Chris can get started with his lesson." Ms. Morning moved to the side so Mr. Chris could have the floor. Mr. Chris acted as if he was washing off all the germs from their hugs as he said, "What's up everybody? Y'all ready to write some more poetry today?" They all responded in sync with a resounding, "Yes, sir!"

Mr. Chris walked to the board and wrote in big letters, the word "METAPHOR." "Today is all about metaphors poets. Metaphors are just like similes. The only difference is you do not use the words LIKE or AS. So yes, you are still comparing two unlike things. You're just taking away the LIKE or AS." Mr. Chris then wrote examples on the board.

Metaphors

Love is a rollercoaster ride.

Life is a box of chocolates.

Flowers are God's art.

The sun is a light bulb.

Joseph's brain is a computer.

The school was a jungle.

The snow was a white blanket.

Time is money.

My dad is a bear.

She is a dancing peacock.

Larry was a pig at lunch.

You are my diamond.

He reminds me of a black panther.

Lebron jumps higher than a Kangaroo.

Usain Bolt is faster than lightning.

My mom is more stubborn than a bull.

"Write down these examples so you can reference them at a later time. Now, look closely at these examples. Do you notice that some of these metaphors are the same sentences I used in my simile examples yesterday? But to make it a metaphor I took away the LIKE or AS. In this situation, I am simply making a direct comparison. Metaphors should come quite easy to you all. Especially being that you are so good at similes. Now you guys raise your hands and share your examples of a metaphor." Their hands went up and their answers came out flying with enthusiasm.

"The wind is nature's whistle."

"Music is therapy."

"The burning bush was a sign."

"Martin King was a lion."

"Rosa Parks was a mountain of determination."

"Children can be parrots."

"Success is an ever changing road."

"Her smile was a bright light."

"The losing team was a sinking ship."

"The house is an igloo inside."

Once everyone shared their examples of metaphors, Mr. Chris said to the class,"Okay everyone let's take a poem break." Mr. Chris pulled a brown journal from his book bag and flipped the pages until he found the poem he wanted to share. "Alright class, this poem is about love. I hope you like it. If you don't just act like you do," he said jokingly.

Home By Chris James

She was my house.
Her love was a roof.
Her belief in me were the walls.
Her eyes were the windows.
I stared in them often
trying to find the answers to love.
She was love.
She was the answer.
My heart was just a blind boy.
Immature, unaware
so much to learn.
I was no different from a rock
head hard
stuck in one place.
My life was a tornado.
It was a chaotic whirl of wind.

She was my anchor
the only reason I didn't float away.
She was a boat.
She moved with the waves
but somehow always was in control.
She reminded me of a church
so full of Holy things
like forgiveness
worship, mercy and love.
I was undeserving of her love
but she still gave.
I guess she knew I needed it.

"That's that poem. I hope y'all liked it." The class clapped and snapped. From the corner of the class Ms. Morning said to Mr. Chris, "Awww that was so sweet." "Yeah Mr. Chris. I liked that. She must be a special girl," Joseph said with a grin as the other kids chuckled. "Mr. Chris got a girlfriend. Mr. Chris got a girlfriend," Ashley sang from the back of the room. The class burst into laughter.

"Okay everybody. Calm down. I won't be doing any more poems about love in this class," Mr. Chris said laughing. "And no, I don't have a girlfriend. I have a wife." He walked away as if he had just said the coolest thing ever and dropped the mic. "Ooh. He sure did tell y'all," Ms. Morning said teasing the class. The kids laughed and turned their attention back to Mr. Chris.

Mr. Chris began writing on the board. "Okay my fellow dudes and dudettes, while I am working on these new examples I need you to talk to one another about the metaphors you heard in my poem." For the next eight minutes, the students went back and forth about what they had just heard in Mr. Chris' poem.

"Cool. Cool. You guys sound good. I am beyond proud that you were able to recognize all the metaphors used in my poem. Now, I want you to check out these sentences on the board. These are examples of metaphors used in popular songs."

Metaphors in Songs

"Baby, you're a firework." -Fireworks, Katy Perry

"She's a little red Corvette." -Little Red Corvette, Prince

"I'm a little teapot." - The Wiggles

"She's a dancing machine." -Jackson 5

"She's a flame." -Fire, Alicia Keys

"You are my sunrise on the darkest day."
- Justin Beiber
"Love is a temple." -One, U3

"You are the thunder and I am the lightning."

-Naturally, Selena Gomez

"My heart's a stereo

it beats for you so listen close." -Maroon 6

"She is my rock." -Plies

"Papa was a rolling stone." -Papa Was A
Rolling Stone, Temptations

"You see. Metaphors are all around you. Figurative language is always being used. You just have to pay attention. The last two days I've had you write poems using the poetic devices we learned but today I won't.

But I do challenge you to write a metaphor poem while you're at home. Everyone in here needs to do it. It'll make you a better writer. Especially you Joe. I heard about that talent show you want to win." Joe shook his head up and down and said, "You already know what's up Mr. Chris. I'll be writing all night long."

"Good. Good. Alright dudes and dudettes. Tomorrow, get ready for more dopeness because like always, it's always more to learn."

Exercise #4- Don't just go to the next chapter. Write your own examples of metaphors and make it a poem. You can do it.

Chapter 5
Use Your Imagination

Thursday seemed to have come so quick. They had made it pass the halfway mark of their week. Mr. Chris had a motto: *If I reach one, my mission is complete.* From the looks of things, he had out done himself. Every kid in the fifth-grade hallway was so in love with poetry and Mr. Chris, especially Joseph.

Joseph woke up that morning, rolled over out of the bed and grabbed his poetry notebook. He hurried to get dressed and ran to the bus stop. Something was different about Joseph today. It wasn't his clothes or shoes. It wasn't his determined attitude. It wasn't his wittiness.

All those things were actually the same. But what was different was what he didn't have. For the first time since Joseph was 7 years old, he was without his rap notebook. He sat at the bus stop writing a new poem, using all the cool figurative language he had learned. It was obvious he had fallen in love with someone new and her name was poetry.

Joseph wrote in his poetry notebook the entire bus ride. While he walked off the bus and down the school hall, he read the sentences over and over to himself. He walked to class and went to his seat and continued writing. He continued writing even after all the other students came in loud and disruptive. He remained focused.

Mr. Chris walked in a few minutes after the bell with a radio in his hand. He greeted everyone with a big hello and hugged Ms. Morning. Mr. Chris whispered to Ms. Morning.

"I see our boy over there focused."

"Yes. He's been writing since he got here."

"Is it a rap or a poem?"

"It's definitely a poem."

"Wow. Our rapper is seeing the light."

Mr. Chris walked over to Joseph and peeked at his notebook. Joseph continued writing, not noticing anything or anyone near him. Mr. Chris tapped him and said, "What you working on, Joe?" Joseph paused slowly as he looked up and replied, "I'm working on a new poem. It's gonna be fire." "Okay, Joe. I'm excited to hear what you got." Mr. Chris walked to the front of the class and wrote in big letters across the whiteboard. PERSONIFICATION.

"What's up poets. Today is the day we will all use our imaginations. You have permission to think outside the box. Today, clocks can talk. Cell phones can call people. Televisions can turn themselves on and off. Doors can close themselves. Ooh, your room can even clean its own self today." The students laughed at Mr. Chris.

"Don't laugh. I'm serious. All this is true. Well not literally speaking but figuratively. Another member of the figurative language family is someone called PERSONIFICATION. Personification is when you use your imagination in writing and give an inanimate object human characteristics. *The refrigerator ate all my food* is an example. *The couch stole my money* is another one. *The clock told me it was time to get out of school. The shoes said,"Ouch! You're squishing me."*

Mr. Chris told the students to take a moment to think about all the things they can do as humans. They began yelling out their basic human characteristics.

"We can run."

"We can laugh."

"We can cook."

"We can read and write."

"We can tie our shoes."

"We can rap."

"We can watch tv."

"We can swim."

"We can whistle."

"We can cry."

"We can dance."

"We can cut grass."

"We can type on computers."

"All these answers are great. Now, all you're doing in personification is making a nonhuman thing do one of these actions. Choose something in the class, in the school, something outside or in your house and make it do something only a human can do." The students raised their hands and like always the answers came flying out.

"The book read itself to me."

"The poem wrote me."

"The pencil wrote a letter to the pen."

"The inflatable thing swam."

"My bed made itself."

"My homework jumped in the trash."

"The trash can ate my homework."

"The computer typed an essay."

"The couch watched TV."

"The TV watched me."

"The pots and pans cooked dinner."

"My lawn mower cut the grass."

"The clouds cried."

"The wind whistled."

"The trees danced in the forest."

One of the students yelled out, "Mr. Chris, this is fun." Mr. Chris smiled and replied, "I agree. You get a chance to really be creative and use your imagination." Mr. Chris walked over to the radio he brought in class. "I am about to play a few songs for you. Each song uses personification. Afterwards as a group, we will identify the use of personification in each. So take notes as needed."

The first song Mr. Chris played was Concrete Jungle by the late Bob Marley.

"No sun will shine in my day today
The high yellow moon won't come out to play
I said darkness has covered my light,
And has changed my day into night, yeah."
-Concrete Jungle, Bob Marley

The second song he played was "Thriller" by the
legendary Michael Jackson. The kids danced in their
seats and sang along like they really knew something
about MJ and his music.

*"You try to scream but terror takes the sound before you
make it*
*You start to freeze as horror looks you right between the
eyes*
You're paralyzed
'Cause this is thriller, thriller night
*And no one's gonna save you from the beast about to
strike."*
-Thriller, Michael Jackson

After that, he played "New York, New York" by Frank
Sinatra. None of the kids knew what they were listening
to.

"These vagabond shoes
Are longing to stray

Right through the very heart of it

New York, New York

I want to wake up in a city

That doesn't sleep"

-New York, New York, Frank Sinatra

Then, Mr. Chris turned on a song by Hip Hop's living legend, Common. The song was called "I Used to Love H.E.R". Everyone listened closely trying to figure out the thing this rapper was personifying.

"I met this girl, when I was ten years old

And what I loved most she had so much soul

She was old school, when I was just a shorty

Never knew throughout my life she would be there for me

On the regular, not a church girl she was secular

Not about the money, those studs was mic checking her

But I respected her, she hit me in the heart."

-I Used to Love H.E.R., Common

When the song was done, Mr. Chris asked, "What was he personifying?" Everyone gave it a shot but no one seemed to guess it correctly. So Mr. Chris happily shared. "He was personifying Hip Hop. He wrote and talked about Hip Hop music as if it was a woman."

Lastly, he played a song by the phenomenal artist, Erykah Badu featuring Common called "Love of My Life". "This last song is very similar to the one you just heard. It's known to be an ode to Hip Hop. This artist is also personifying Hip Hop. But this artist wrote about Hip Hop as if it was a man.

"I met him when I was a
A little girl, he gave me
He gave me poetry
He was my first
But in my heart I knew I
Wasn't the only one
'Cause when the tables turned
He had to break, but...

Whenever I got lonely

Or needed some advice

He gave me his shoulder

His words were very nice"

-Love of My Life, Erykah Badu

Once he played all the songs for the students, he put the radio away and requested everyone's undivided attention for he was going to share a personification poem. "So as you probably expected, I am going to share a poem using personification. I will not say what the thing is that I am personifying. You must listen closely and take your guess."

A Readers Love by Chris James

I can't put you down.

You are so full of excitement.

You always know exactly what to say

Full of all the right words.

Because of you,

I write words.

Since I was a child
you have scratched my curiosity
pushed me to expand my vocabulary.
I remember getting my first card to come into
your house
so I could finally check you out.
I was told not to judge you by your cover
but instead
by the content of your characters,
your plot, exposition, your rising action,
the climax and resolution.
When I was unable to go anywhere
you took me on adventures.
You took me places I never imagined.
You made me imagine.
Your pages are worth every turn.
I am grateful for you.
You will forever have a place on the shelf
of my heart.
Sincerely, a reader.

The class snapped and clapped for Mr. Chris once he completed his poem. He asked the class, "What was I personifying?" After the first three students guessed incorrectly, Joseph raised his hand and said the correct answer loudly, "A book. You were personifying a book." Everyone else said in unison, "Aaaaawwww." They realized right then all the clues Mr. Chris had given in his poem that clearly alluded to this answer. "Joe, you are correct. Good job young sir."

Mr. Chris wanted to waste no more time so he instructed everyone to grab a piece of paper and pencil. "Alright class, choose a topic and personify it. Give that thing human like characteristics. In order for this to work, you must be very detailed and descriptive in your writing. I will write on the board a few topics you can choose from." Mr. Chris wrote the topics on the board and shortly after, everyone was busy writing.

Topics

Love   Bullying

Depression

Pain

Happiness   Cigarettes

Nature

Technology

War   Money

Mr. Chris walked around the room to make sure everyone was focused and writing. He looked over and noticed even Ms. Morning was writing this time. He noticed Joseph smiling as he wrote. Mr. Chris knew some good poems were being born. The timer on Mr. Chris' phone went off and writing time was up. It was time to share the masterpieces yet again. "I'll go first," Ms. Morning anxiously volunteered.

Ms. Morning's Personification Poem

She is a mother to many.

I've watched her change the colors

of leaves on trees like diapers on babies.

She is winter, spring, summer and autumn.

She is the reason for the flowers' blossom.

She is every bit of awesome.

She is green grass.

She is rain and lightning

sunshine and bright skies.

She is the mountains and the valleys.

She is the fish and lake they swim in.

The birds and the trees.

The honey and the bees.

She is mother to all.

Darla Jenkins

10/19/17

Ms. Morning's 5th Grade

Love Is...

We are all made in the name of it.

It conquers all.

Hate stands no chance against it.

It is water to fire.

It lives in your heart even when anger tries to
move in.
It sweeps you off your feet
and makes you fall in deep.
This is the best place to swim.
When you see it
hold on to it and never let go.

Chassity James
10/19/17
Ms. Morning's 5th Grade

War Poem

He tears countries apart.
He causes chaos and fights for no real reason.
Many have lost their lives because of him.
He is bloody, unforgiving and permanent.
It is no erasing the damage he causes.
Our history books praise him
while he awaits the next opportunity
to fight for more power
by ending more lives.

Terry St. Claire
10/19/17
Ms. Morning's 5th Grade

The Smokey Stinky Things

Smoke me. Smoke me.
And so many people do it.
He is addictive.

My parents won't put him out.
He is a fire that is burning their lungs.
I see him in the ashtray
and the ground in my neighborhood.
I see the older kids trying to be cool
by smoking him.
He is dangerous.
And because of him
Cancer will soon be knocking
and it will not be delivering any good news.

They went through three whole tables and everyone's poem was amazing. It was Joseph's turn. He stood up,

walked to the front of class just as he did the times
before, and he shared again with expression.

Joseph Hardaway
10/19/17
Ms. Morning's 5th Grade

Money Money Money

In 1993, the rap group known as
Wu Tang Clan rapped about it in their song
C.R.E.A.M.
It rules everything around us.
People will do anything for it.
It's green and will make you mean.
It'll change your entire life.
It will make you do wrong
and avoid doing right.
It can make you happy
but it can also drive you crazy.
It has the ability to buy you nice things.
If I could I'd grow it on trees.
I can hear it now

saying "Spend me. Spend me."
It dances in your pockets anxious
to be traded for material things.
But we hate to let it go
but we love getting mo',
I mean more.
Just so we can go spend it again
at the closest store.

Joseph ended his poem and waited for the applause. Everyone clapped and shouted for him as he dabbed and walked back to his seat. "Good job Joe. I liked that joint a lot. I almost threw a dollar at you," Mr. Chris complimented Joseph from the corner of the room. "Alright class, we got a few more poets and it'll be a wrap for today." The rest of the students shared over the next ten minutes. Once they were finished, Mr. Chris commended the entire class for doing so great over the last week. "Class, we did good work today. Tomorrow is Friday. Friday is my favorite day so we will be talking about my favorite figurative language family member.

Go home and write some more poems and I'll see y'all tomorrow. Deuces." The bell rang. Mr. Chris grabbed his bag and exited the room.

Exercise #5- Write you a personification poem.
You can do it.
Use your imagination.

Chapter 6

Poets Paint Pictures with Purpose

Fridays can be full of fun especially when words wage
wars on paper. In other words, it was Friday and the day
was about to be filled with great poetry. Mr. Chris and
the class started the day off with the category game.
Together they sang, "This is the game of concentration.
No repeats or hesitations. Category is ..." Mr. Chris
chose the category. "The category is words that start

with the letter P." The students used every P word they could think of. Pumpkin, peach, paradise, Paris, prey, preacher, pie, pudding, possum, park, parrot, pink, party, pizza. They went around in a circle until people started hesitating and repeating answers -- eliminating themselves from the game.

"The next category is saying a complete sentence that uses at least three words with the same letter. Go." The circle started getting smaller and smaller by the second because absolutely no one got it right.

"Guys, this is easy. Everyone go to your seat. Let's begin today's lesson." Mr. Chris wrote a word on the board. ALLITERATION. "We will be learning about another member of the figurative language family. His name is ALLITERATION. Some may call it the tongue twister. I call it fun, fun and more fun. Alliteration is the repetition of initial sounds or letters in the same sentence. Check out my examples up here."

Alliteration

Ladies love laughing.

Boys bounce basketballs.

Alex ate applesauce with an alligator.

Felix fell on the football field.

Girls are goofy and gossip.

The green grass grew gradually.

My dirty dog digs ditches.

Lions lie lazily in lakes.

Walls whisper words in the wind.

Poets paint pictures with pens and pencils on paper.

Jordan jumped over the jungle gym.

The cats kicked it with the kittens.

Once Mr. Chris finished sharing, Joseph was already raising his hand to share his examples.

"Rappers write rhymes.

Students study social studies and science.

Teachers talk to toddlers.

My mom makes macaroni and cheese."

Mr. Chris looked at Joseph with a look of satisfaction. "This is pretty easy," Joseph boasted. "Yes, it is, Joe. It's not supposed to be hard at all. It's fun." After Joseph shared, everyone had their hands up ready to show that they also understood alliteration. And the examples came flying like tennis balls.

"Mary made a mountain out of muffins."

"Harold had a whole head of hair."

"Lisa listens to Larry."

"Joseph joined the jury."

"Ms. Morning made me move."

"The queen quietly questioned the results of the quiz."

"The whale wasted water."

"Ducks dive deep."

"Tigers tease turtles."

"Felicia found frogs in the fridge."

"Beyonce bowls balls in her backyard."

"Jay Z jogged in the jungle on a journey."

"The chicken chased the chihuahua."

"Paul played ping pong."

"Snakes slither slowly."

"Students shouldn't sit in silence when confused."

"You guys are making today real easy for me. I don't even have to teach because you comprehend so well." Everyone received Mr. Chris' compliment as they patted themselves on the back. "Who thinks they can write an entire poem using alliteration?"

"Me, me, me," the students all replied together. "Okay. Okay. I believe you. Well before you do that I will share a poem written by one of my favorite poets, Drekkia Writes."

Drekkia's Personification Poem

Impractical people practice this art of perfection

In opposition, poet's pencil precision on pieces of

paper

People pursue this pursuit of this illusion of

perfect

Picture a person

The product of imperfect

Sleeping with serpents

See, some people would rather pay for redemption

instead of praying for mercy

Placing a price on my perspective

What's the plight of the people?

Polluted perceptions

Punish populations of a poisonous public

So, what's the purpose of privilege if the problems

are plenty?

Positive permutation

Pretenders posing

They're phony

With facades of pandemonium

Proclaiming pleasure in pity
Pressing to be pretty
With personalities equivalent to a penny.

Mr. Chris closed the book expressing that he was finished and everyone sat there with their mouths wide open. "Wow! That was goooooood," Chassity said with her jaw still dropped. The other students agreed. "That sounded like a rap," Joseph said to Mr. Chris as he stood up with his hands on his head as if his mind was just blown away. "That's what I've been trying to explain to you all this time Joe. Rap is poetry and poetry is rap. They are one," Mr. Chris replied with passion. "I believe you, Mr. Chris. This alliteration stuff is pretty cool."

Mr. Chris went to the board and instructed everyone to write their own alliteration poems. "Don't worry so much about a topic this time but I do want each alliteration example to make sense and be complete sentences. So just write. Make your poem just as great as the one I shared." Ms. Morning turned on some John

Coltrane music and the students began writing for the next twenty minutes.

Joseph sat in his desk rocking his head as if he was listening to music. Alliteration seemed to have a rhythm that made him want to move. The timer on Mr. Chris'

phone went off and it was time to share poems for the day. "Here we go. Y'all know what time it is. Time to share those poems." Mr. Chris told everyone that this time they had to come to the front of the room. Again, they started by tables. The poems began.

Rhyleigh Plummer
10/20/17
Ms. Morning's 5th Grade

My Dad

I watched my dad do duties in the dawn of day.
He cut the grass that grew gradually from the ground.
He still finds time to teach the tennis team.
My dad is old but operates
like an owl outside at night.
My brother bothers balls in my dad's big basket.
In the mornings my dad, the coach,
drinks coffee from a cool cup on the counter.
He is so super smart and strong.

His head holds history like holy books.
He gives me and my mommy money
to make memories at the mall.
My dad's tough truck can tow an entire tower of
toys.
He drives it fast and furious with his friends on
Fridays.
They sit in the backyard beneath the barn behind the
barbecue grill.
My dad is the best boy and can balance a baseball on
his brain.
The end.

Henry McAdoo
10/20/17
Ms. Morning's 5th Grade

The Teacher Lady

The lazy lady hasn't cleaned lately.
She sleeps soundly in the summer.
The cats and kittens cook her cookies
while the wind whispers
and clouds clap from rain roaring
she continues snoring.

The precipitation keeps peacefully pouring.

People pass her porch with purpose.

No one seems to notice she's been absent.

Everyone's focused on reasons to rush

and run not realizing that life is not a race.

She awakes and sits silently as the summer season

slowly seeps.

Like a snake the school semester will slither soon and

she is in no rush for crowds of crazy kids crawling

all over the class.

All the students had awesome poems. Mr. Chris was again proud of the young poets progress. Friday was turning out to be everything he could have hoped for. "This day can't possibly get any better," Mr. Chris said jokingly knowing Joseph would disagree. "It can definitely get better bearded poet. You forgot I haven't gone yet." Joseph walked to the front of the class and let the words flow.

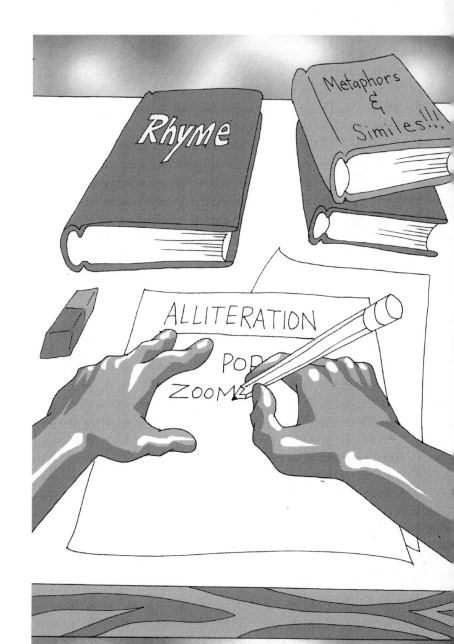

Joseph Hardaway

10/20/17

Ms. Morning's 5th Grade

The Art I Am

I am the wind beneath the wings of words.

I've sang songs to save shallow souls.

I am the moaning music made on the moon

that the wolves howl to.

I am a poem on the front page of a newspaper.

I am a Picasso picture painted on the pavement.

I create conversations with colors from crayons kids

can't seem to keep from crashing like cars.

I heal hurting hearts.

I've traveled on trains from Toronto to Tanzania from

Texas to Tennessee

to see the sun shine over the sea.

If I was a day I'd be Monday.

In the morning I'd make magic with the moments.

I'd bring the blue birds back to my basement to sing

background

for blues tunes.

If I was a paint brush I'd stroke splashes of acrylic
paint on the canvas.

Actually, I am all these things.

I am art.

Joseph looked at Mr. Chris awaiting his approval. All the students clapped and made noise for Joseph's poem. Ms. Morning smiled while telling Joseph good job. Mr. Chris walked up to Joseph and said, "Now Joe, that right there is the best rap you've ever written." Joseph smiled and replied, "Thanks. This was actually a poem." Mr. Chris smiled and agreed. "You're right. It was definitely a poem." Mr. Chris wrapped up the class with words of encouragement and told everyone to have a lit Friday and to be ready for next week. There was a little more to learn. But the end of Mr. Chris' stay was near.

Exercise #5- Write five examples of alliteration
and share them aloud.

Chapter 7

Making Noises and Exaggerating

Monday, Monday, Monday. It was Monday which is everyone's absolute favorite day. It was such a good day that you could hear cars going vroom vroom all across the street. You could even hear the horns honking. Beeeeep. Beeeep. The students were so excited about Monday you could hear them dropping their books from rushing. Splat! Flop! The students ran in Ms. Morning's class before the roosters could cock a doodle doo. Ms.

Morning walked in and noticed the class was ready to work with Mr. Chris. They knew his visit was coming to an end and they wanted to enjoy every minute with him. Brrrriiiiiiiiiiiiinnnnnngggg! The bell rang and Mr. Chris walked in. Bang! He closed the door.

"What's up poets? Y'all look like you're ready to take on the world." The room was so silent you could hear a fly breathing. Bzzzzzz. "Joseph ran up to Mr. Chris and hugged him. "We just ready to hang with you bearded poet. We know you leaving us soon." The students looked at Mr. Chris with their puppy dog eyes. "Aaaawww y'all stop before y'all make me cry a man tear." He pretended to sob and boo-hoo. Everyone ran up to Mr. Chris and hugged him. You could hear all the bodies shuffling and feet pitter-patter as everyone tried to get their hug.

"Alright. Get off of me," Mr. Chris begged with a smile on his face. "We are about to play a game. Boys against girls. Today we will be doing two things but the first is all about sounds." Mr. Chris wrote a big strange word on the board. ONOMATOPOEIA. Everyone looked at the word trying to figure out how to say it and what exactly it meant. Mr. Chris looked at the class and said the word slowly.

"On-o-mat-o-poe-ia." He had everyone practice saying this new word about fifteen more times. "I know this is a weird word but it's fun. Onomatopoeia is the forming of words to describe a sound. You see onomatopoeia in comic books all the time. For example: pow, wham, boom, zap, poof, boing. The list goes on. The game we are about to play is all about sounds. Whichever team can give me the most words that describe sounds wins. Girls and boys, you must say your sound and then write it on the board." The game begun and they hurried to share their answers.

Girls

Ice in glass— ting ting ting

yummm

Rain— beat, drip, drop, drum, Kerplunk, lash, patter, pelt, pink, plop, ponk, rat-a-tat tat, rattle, shatter, slap, slash, splash, splat, splatter, slosh, splish, splosh, thump

ahhhhhhh

Bees— hum, buzz, zooom

Moo

Ducks— quack

Soda— ssssss

sizzle

slurp

Click, Clack

uh-oh

Excitement— yoo-hoo, yahoo, yeeha, yippee

Horn — beeeep, honk, BLURRT, HON-NK H- HONK-K,

HONK-A H-HONK, HON-N-N-K- KHON-N-K H-HON-

N-K, AU-OOGA

Clock-tick, tock, tic toc, ding, ding, cuckcoo

Boys

Snakes — hiss, rattle, slither

Alien— nanoo nanoo, beeepbop, earrrthling

Bigfoot— fum fum fum, grrrrr

Ghost— boo, oooohh

cock-a- doodle-doo

Sick — Achoo, Arf, Barf, Bleh, Brr, Choo, Cough, Eugh, Hachoo Splutter

Laugh — Cackle, Chortle, Giggle, Guffaw, Haha, Hehe

Sleep — Snore, Zzz

Boots — schloop schloop, thump thump

yikes

Laser — pew, pew

Pencil sharpener — grind, grind, whizz, gweeze

-Paddle boat

Kloosh-kloosh-kloosh-kloosh Gloosh-gloosh-gloosh-gloosh

Dogs- woof, woof, urff urff

Cats- Meow

"And time. Time is up. Everyone go to your seats. That was a good round. I need a drum roll please." The students made a loud drum roll with their feet on the floor and hands tapping on the tables. Mr. Chris turned on his radio announcement voice. "The winners of the first annual onomatopoeia contest aaaarrrrrreeee the girls." The girls jumped up in excitement and the boys yelled for a rematch while others slumped in their seats and crossed their arms.

"Hey boys, don't be sore losers. You win some and you lose some but you live to fight another day," Mr. Chris said quoting Craig's father from the classic movie FRIDAY starring rapper, Ice Cube. "I won't make you write onomatopoeia poems today but everyone check out this one I wrote. He passed out the poem and allowed everyone to read it to themselves.

My Sound Poem
by Chris James

I was dribbling the ball
thump thump
as I ran down the court and the clock was winding
down
The basketball went swish
The crowd roared.
The buzzer went off.
All of a sudden I heard a bang at the door

and my alarm went off
vbeep vbeep.
I woke up and realized it was a dream.

"Alright. Moving on. The second lesson today is all about exaggerating. Which is exactly what some of the boys are doing right now. Sit up guys. Let's get hype. The next figurative language member is HYPERBOLE. It's pronounced hi-per-bu-lee. Hyperbole is an exaggerated statement. Check out my examples.

It was so hot she melted.

I can eat a whole cow.

He jumped higher than a shooting star.

I can sleep for an entire year.

She was one hundred feet tall.

The dog barked a hole in the wall.

You always have a million excuses.

Keep eating and you'll gain a thousand pounds.

It took you forever to get here.

You cooked enough to end world hunger.

I have a ton of homework.

I'm going to freeze to death in here.

You notice how my examples seemed to be impossible or just a bit much? That's what hyperbole is. It's all about being big and very extra. Your turn. Try it."

"That's enough water to fill the ocean."

"I love you to the moon and back."

"The elevator is slower than a snail."

"Her hair is longer than the Nile river."

"He is stronger than one hundred bears."

"The track team ran faster than the speed of light."

"I can smell your breath from a mile away."

"I'd jump in the ocean to find your tears."

"The baby weighed a ton."

"My dad never sleeps."

"My mom practically lives on Facebook."

"Mr. Jenkins never stops talking."

"Everybody knows that."

"This is the longest test ever."

"She is thin enough to fit in the key hole."

"I'd die to hug Beyonce."

"This homework is killing me."

"My papa is older than dinosaurs."

"Your smile erases all the world's worry."

The students gave some really great examples of hyperbole. Mr. Chris knew they wouldn't have a problem with that. After all, exaggerating is what children do for a living. "Good stuff. By now, you guys know the drill. Time to write your poems and share. The writing commenced. Over the next thirty minutes Mr. Chris and Ms. Morning walked around and read each students poem.

Lisa Muhummad
10/23/17
Ms. Morning's 5th Grade

A Love Like This

I love you around the moon and back.
The sight of you makes me fly.

Or maybe that's just the butterflies you make
visit my belly.
Your corny jokes make even the Grinch laugh.
He laughs so hard he turns blue.
Your smile is so bright that even the sun gets
jealous.

Malachi Jenkins
10/23/17
Ms. Morning's 5th Grade

Mama's Boy

My mom's hugs are softer than clouds.
She cooks us million dollar meals.
When we are sick she turns flips to get us
better.
She is absolutely the best mother ever.

Chrissette James

10/23/17

Ms. Morning's 5th Grade

My Brother

My brother is so clumsy
he has broken every plate in our house.
He trips every time he walks.
When he goes to heaven I am sure he will
find a way to break the gate.
Just yesterday, he ruined my entire life.
I can still hear my favorite mug crashing on the
kitchen floor.
Clink clink, smash.
Ugh. I'm so angry.

Joseph Hardaway

10/23/17

Ms. Morning's 5th Grade

Hip Hop Vol. 1

Hip Hop has saved more lives
than all the Marvel heroes combined.

Hip Hop moves the world from side to side.
I play my music so loud that even the angels can hear it.
I rap so tight that my dog starts doing the floss and hitting that name nae.
My lyrics flow like rivers which means a boat can float on my rhymes.
I got vibranium in my veins.
I might take a flight to Wakanda tomorrow night.
When I get famous my stage will have enough light to brighten the entire world.

Everyone finished writing their poem. Joseph sat in his seat smiling. He was so excited about his writing. He wanted to share but Mr. Chris already said that they wouldn't have time today. Mr. Chris walked over to check on Joseph.

"What you smiling about dude?"

"My poem is pretty dope."

"Yeah it is. I read it."

"Let me read it to you so you can really hear it."

"Joe, if you read yours everybody will want to read theirs too. We don't have time."

Joseph sighed. Mr. Chris asked everyone to put down their pens and pencils so he could wrap up for the day. "Today was good. Tomorrow and Wednesday will be my last days. Let's have a great time. See y'all tomorrow." Mr. Chris grabbed his bag and headed out for the day. The students were beyond ready for the next day to come.

Exercise #7- Write the sounds you hear on television, in your house or at the park. Also write examples of hyperbole. Exaggerate!

Chapter 8
Old People Be Like & Double Meanings

Joseph's dad dropped him off at the school early. Like they say, the early bird gets the worm. Joseph walked in class ready to seize the day. Mr. Chris was already seizing it. Joseph walked in to a board full of phrases Mr. Chris had written down. Mr. Chris stood there writing and dancing with his music blasting from the computer speakers.

"Mr. Chris, what you working on?"

"Joe, you almost scared me. What's up with you? You're early."

"My bad, Mr. Chris. Didn't mean to startle you. My dad and I went for donuts before school so he dropped me off early."

"That's pretty cool. You bring me some donuts?"

"Not this time. I ate them all."

"Next time don't leave me out."

"I won't. I promise. What's all this on the board?"

"That's today's lesson. You ever heard of an adage?"

"A what?"

"An adage. It's a proverb or short saying that usually expresses truth or wisdom. Think about it as something the Wizard of Oz or your grandparents might say."

"Awwww okay. Like, 'An apple a day keeps the doctor away'?"

"Exactly. That's an adage. We will talk more about it in a minute. Let me finish writing these right quick before the bell rings."

Joseph went to his seat and started writing a poem while Mr. Chris finished preparing for today's lesson. Ten minutes went by and the bell rang. The class came running in. "Everyone take a seat. Let's get to business. Check out the board. These are what you call ADAGES. An adage is an old saying. Write these down."

Adage Examples

Birds of a feather flock together.

Opposites attract.   Don't judge a book by its cover.

The clothes don't make the man.

The early bird gets the worm.

Better late than never.   Nothing ventured, nothing gained.

You are never too old to learn.

You can't teach an old dog new tricks.

A rolling stone gathers no moss.

Stop and smell the roses.   Strike while the iron is hot.

Look before you leap.   Many hands make light work.

Two heads are better than one.

Too many cooks spoil the broth.   Measure twice, cut once.

You can't have your cake and eat it too.

A bird in the hand is worth two in the bush

Don't count your chickens before they're hatched.

Better safe than sorry.

Curiosity killed the cat.

What you don't know can't hurt you.

Seek and ye shall find.

There's no such thing as a free lunch.

The best things in life are free.

Two wrongs don't make a right.

Practice makes perfect.

Don't put all your eggs in one basket.

A penny saved is a penny earned.

Waste not, want not.

When the going gets tough, the tough get going.

Actions speak louder than words.

Don't cut off your nose to spite your face.

No man is an island.   A watched pot never boils.

Don't jump out of the frying pan and into the fire.

Don't cry over spilt milk.   You are what you eat.

Don't bite the hand that feeds you.

Beggars can't be choosers.

Don't put the cart before the horse.

You can lead a horse to water, but you can't make him drink.

People who live in glass houses shouldn't throw stones.

Do unto others as you would have them do unto you.

Honesty is the best policy.

There's no time like the present.

Don't put off till tomorrow what you can do today.

There's no place like home.   Home is where the heart is.

Time flies when you're having fun.

A chain is only as strong as its weakest link.

All that glitters is not gold.   Silence is golden.

The pen is mightier than the sword.

A picture is worth a thousand words.

After several minutes of reading over the examples of adages, Mr. Chris explained further. "Adages are a lot like quotes. They are really good to use as openers for your writing. Adages make readers want to know more about the character or theme. They carry messages that many people can relate to and understand. And they are just beautiful arrangements of words. Check out this example. When I was younger my father used to tell me don't judge a book by its cover.

If I read this sentence in a poem I would automatically know what it means and I would be interested in knowing more about the storyline or plot."

The students took note of Mr. Chris' advice. Mr. Chris went on to say, "I won't stay too long on this because I have one more thing I'd like to cover today." He went to the board again, erased some of the adages and wrote the word, IDIOM and its definition.

Idiom- a phrase that has both a literal and a figurative meaning.

"An idiom is a phrase that doesn't actually have a definition but rather a general understanding behind it.

Check out these examples. The examples are of course the figurative meaning. We will discuss the literal meaning."

A penny for your thoughts
"It is a way of asking what someone is thinking."

Actions speak louder than words
"It's saying that people's intentions can be judged better by what they do rather than what they say."

Add insult to injury
"This means to make a situation worse than it already is."

At the drop of a hat
"To do without any hesitation."

Back to the drawing board
"This has to do with when you start over after failing."

Ball is in your court
"The choice or next move is up to you."

Barking up the wrong tree
"You are accusing the wrong person or going in the wrong direction."

Beat around the bush
"You are avoiding the truth or speaking indirectly."

Best of both worlds
"You're getting all the advantages."

Best thing since sliced bread
"A good invention or idea."

Bite off more than you can chew
"To take on a task too big."

Can't judge a book by its cover
"You can't measure something or someone by appearance only."

Costs an arm and a leg
"Something is expensive."

Cross that bridge when you come to it

"Deal with it when it arrives or becomes relevant."

Cry over spilt milk

"To complain about something from the past."

Curiosity killed the cat

"Being too nosey can sometimes get you in trouble."

Don't count your chickens before the eggs have hatched

"Don't make plans for something that might not happen."

Don't give up the day job

"You're not very good at something."

Don't put all your eggs in one basket

"Do not put all your resources in one possibility."

Feel a bit under the weather

"To feel sick."

Hit the nail on the head

"To do or say something exactly right."

Hit the sack / sheets / hay

"To go to bed."

Jump on the bandwagon

"To do something because everyone else is doing it."

Kill two birds with one stone

"To accomplish two tasks at one time."

Let the cat out of the bag

"To tell information that was supposed to be a secret."

Once in a blue moon

"It doesn't happen often."

Piece of cake

"It is easy."

Steal someone's thunder

"To take the credit for something someone else did."

Take with a grain of salt

"Don't take it too seriously."

Taste of your own medicine

"To experience what you usually do to others."

Straight from the horse's mouth

"To hear something from the main source."

They spent almost the entire class talking about idioms. There were so many examples and it was still more Mr. Chris could have talked about. "I know that was a lot. If you paid close attention, you'd notice that some of the idioms were also adages. That goes to show that adages and idioms are actually cousins. Idioms can be used in the same way as adages in your writing." Teaching about both adages and idioms in the same day was like killing two birds with one stone. Everything was connecting so perfectly. "Tomorrow is my last day." The students all responded, "Aaaaaawww."

"Don't be sad. I'll see you again. Tomorrow is going to be the wrap up. We are going to incorporate everything I've taught you over these last seven days so go home and study. Also, I want you to come prepared to express yourselves, to paint your thoughts and emotions on paper with words."

Mr. Chris went around the room shaking everyone's hands and giving out hugs before he left for the day. The day was over for Mr. Chris but he left feeling full. He was full of joy because so many young people had become young poets.

Exercise #8- Go back to a previous poem you wrote and add one adage and one idiom.

Chapter 9
Just Write

Education means nothing without application. In other words, all Mr. Chris had taught these students would be a waste if they didn't actually apply the information. Today, they'd put the rubber to the road or in this case the pen to paper. The last day was here. Mr. Chris walked into the class a little after the bell rang. The music was jamming like it was a party going on. The students were passing around what seemed to be a large card. Ms. Morning turned down the music once she noticed Mr. Chris had come in. "Everybody, Mr. Chris is in the building," Ms. Morning shouted to the class as they shifted their attention to him. The students ran up to hug Mr. Chris.

"We will miss you."

"Does this have to be your last day?"

"Will you come back?"

"Mr. Chris, you're the best."

"Can I touch your beard one last time?"

"Children sit down. Stop being so dramatic. Y'all acting like I'm moving to Mars or something. We family for life now. Y'all can email me, hit me on Facebook or Instagram. And yes, I follow back." Everyone went back to their seat, backs hunched over expressing their sadness. Mr. Chris wrote his social media and website on the board.

Instagram- @chrisjamesjourney
Facebook- The Chris James Journey
Website- www.TheChrisJamesJourney.com

"I am excited about today. Everything we learned over the last seven days comes to this important moment. Today, you all will be writing free verse poems that express your thoughts, opinions and emotions. No rules. All I ask is that you be honest and use all that I've taught you. Paint pictures with your words."

Mr. Chris walked to the computer and pulled up a video on Youtube. It was a video of a poem written and performed by Sabrina Benaim entitled *Explaining My Depression to My Mother*. He then had everyone focus their attention to the video. "This poem is great to watch because she is going to use almost every form of figurative language. When you hear examples, I want you guys to take note of it. Once the video is done, I want you to raise your hand and tell me what figurative language you heard." He pressed play and Ms. Morning hit the light switch. As the video played, you could see the thrill in their eyes. They felt so accomplished being able to recognize this stuff.

The video ended and their hands went up. Each student gave examples from the poem. They broke down the video like they were scientists. And at this point they were. Scientists of poetry of course. "Okay, cool, cool. I see y'all showing out. Let's hear one more poem before I release you guys to write. This is one of my original poems. It's called *Don't Fit In*.

Don't Fit In

by Chris James

My daughter, Rhyleigh, says to me
"Daddy I don't wanna go to school anymore
because the other kids laugh at me and say I got
a light bulb head."
So I told her
Do unto others as you would have them do unto
you.
Silence is golden
Don't allow their tainted tongues to tremble
or trouble your throne
because remember, you are a queen
so don't ever attempt to metamorph into
metaphors
and compare yourself to people or things that you
aren't like

because you are a
CIRCLE
well rounded, 360 degrees of perfection
and society's perception of what beauty is
will attempt to anorex your self-esteem
until it's nothing of you left.
Maybelline will attempt to make you believe
that you need make-up to cover the girl you are
to become a woman of worth.
And boys will attempt to use your beauty as
target practice
aiming to convince their peers and themselves that
they are
the men that they have yet to learn how to be.
So keep your eye on their bull.
I
just need YOU
to be prepared
Because when you are in positions of power
peasants will always be on the prowl for your
place
but remind them that you are irreplaceable.

Stand your ground.

Don't be moved by their bulldozers of bitterness
attempting to Twin Tower collapse your
confidence.

Use their sticks and stones as stepping stones
for your stairway to success.

Shine bright like a diamond.

Yes, you are the hardest and most precious
substance on Earth

but you are still as soft as sunny Sunday
mornings.

It's alright to allow tears to leak from the
windows to your soul.

Cry yourself a river

but always remember to smile

because your smile

takes fresh breaths of air from lungs

and resuscitates life into lost and lifeless souls.

Your smile speaks the language of happy.

You give birth to better days

just by simply waking up in the morning.

You are important and you already matter

just as much as matter
and oxygen and carbon dioxide and the ozone.
You are a pot of gold.
Your thoughts are winning lottery tickets.
Your mind is worth millions

so don't ever waste your time
I mean your money
I mean your mind
worrying about those other kids
because remember,
you are a queen
so there is never a need to metamorph into
metaphors and compare yourself to people or
things you aren't like
because you are a CIRCLE
well rounded, 360 degrees of perfection.
You will never fit in
so get used to standing out.

Mr. Chris finished and their hands went up again, ready
to answer. They were on it. Collectively, they named all
of the similes, metaphors, alliteration, personification,

adages and hyperboles in the poem. Mr. Chris was pleased. It was writing time again, for the last time. "Good job class. So, here we are. I shared those two poems so you'd have a real idea of what all figurative language sounded like in a poem. This is the moment I've been waiting on. I want you to write the best poems ever today. Express yourself in color. Let's take a few minutes to popcorn out some potential topics to write about." As the students called out topics, Mr. Chris wrote them on the board.

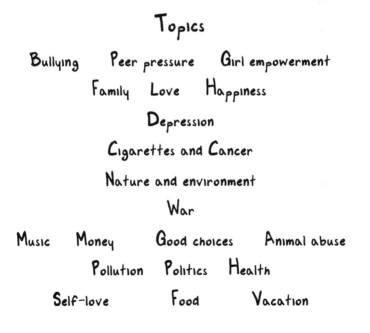

Topics

Bullying   Peer pressure   Girl empowerment
Family   Love   Happiness
Depression
Cigarettes and Cancer
Nature and environment
War
Music   Money   Good choices   Animal abuse
Pollution   Politics   Health
Self-love   Food   Vacation

They filled the board with ideas. Joseph raised his hand and asked, "Can we use more than one of these topics?"

"Yes, you can. If it makes sense for you to combine several topics then go for it. Let's get to writing young poets. You have twenty minutes." Mr. Chris walked around for a few minutes encouraging the students. "Don't focus so much on being right. Just write." He even gave some of the students examples of figurative language to use in their poems. Afterwards, he went to the corner to start writing his own.

Joseph sat there focused as he always did. He was writing up a storm. While many students were still on a half page, Joseph was already on the back of his paper. He obviously had a lot to say.

The writing time had expired. The pens had spilled their share of ink. The paper had served its purpose and became the art it was born to be. Poems had been birthed and the young writers in Ms. Morning's fifth grade class were the proud creators. For the last time Mr.

Chris made the announcement for the poets to share. Each student seemed to have a different type of confidence this time. They were prepared and pleased. Each student stepped up to the front of the class and poured out their souls.

These last moments with Mr. Chris had turned out to be something special. Some students cried during their poems because they were so connected to the topics. Some students were full of joy while others were passionate and expressed anger. Mr. Chris allowed it all to be spilled on the page and the stage. The most beautiful thing about this day was nobody was judged for their honest poems.

Joseph sat in the back of the room waiting patiently for his chance to go. He wanted to share last because his poem wouldn't just be a regular poem. It was more personal this time. Joseph walked to the front of the room. He looked at Mr. Chris. Mr. Chris looked at him. Joseph scanned the room to make sure everyone was paying attention. Then he began sharing his poem.

Joseph Hardaway
10/23/17
Ms. Morning's 5th Grade

MY NEW LOVE

Never judge a book by its cover.
When I met you
I thought we had nothing in common.
You were so full of new ideas.
But I was content with my current content.
I thought to myself
Who are you to offer any edits
to my already perfectly penned masterpiece.
I allowed you a seat at the table of my mind.
I don't regret it.
A bearded man told me you could change my life
if I let it.
I let you.
You are perfect
You give my pen and pencil purpose.
You are deep, beyond the surface.
You are a party
and I'd dance to your rhythm.

Your rhyme is like a drum set.

I'm in love with your beat.

You make me move my feet.

You are the heat and the water.

You bring the cold and the fire.

You are art.

You hang on the walls of my heart.

You are the best part.

You are like a new language.

Your words flow like rivers.

I'd gladly float on your every sentence.

Somehow you make the world go round.

You are the mother to music.

Your lyrics are the foundation

Thank you for the inspiration.

Thank you for filling my pages.

Dear poetry,

thank you.

Joseph finished and the class erupted into celebration.
He remained at the front soaking it all in. Mr. Chris

smiled big as he walked over to Joseph and picked him up off his feet. Josephs' feet dangled in the air as Mr. Chris celebrated him, "Joe, you got flow. You got the poetry glow. You are a real deal rapper poet now." Joseph smiled. He was so happy that Mr. Chris had finally validated his talent.

Ms. Morning came to the front of the room and demanded everyone's attention. "Before this fantastic day ends and all this magic fades, we have a special announcement we'd like to share." Once Ms. Morning gave her signal, the students grabbed balloons from the closet and gifts they had prepared that were hidden in their desk. Ms. Morning held up the large card they had created earlier. Then all the students read it aloud together.

"Mr. Chris, we would like to thank you for visiting our class. You have truly impacted us all. Like you once said we are officially family forever now. We love you."

Mr. Chris blushed and seemed to have a drop of water in his eyes. He wiped his face and looked away. They then presented him with their personalized letters and gifts. Amongst the gifts were flowers, balloons, fruit snacks, hot chips, a necklace made of sea shells and a picture of the entire class in a frame. Everyone had shared their gifts. Mr. Chris couldn't have been any happier in this moment. The day had been topped off with whipped cream and a cherry on top. Mr. Chris prepared to wrap up and head out. Joseph jumped up and shouted, "I got something to say." He walked back to the front of the class.

"I want to say thank you Mr. Chris for challenging me. You made me realize that in order to be a great rapper, I must also learn and value the art of poetry. With that being said in the talent show I won't only rap. I'll be performing a poem too. And I'd like you to be there."

"I appreciate you for accepting the challenge. Always remember, a poem is never done. You can always add more. You can always grow. The same goes for life.

You will always be a student to life but you have to be willing to receive the lesson. And in these past two weeks you showed this to be true. I'm proud to know you, Joe. I'd be honored to come watch you in the talent show."

Mr. Chris and Joseph shook hands and hugged. The bell rang and everyone else in the class joined in for their final hug too. The students disappeared into the hallway. Mr. Chris had completed his mission and Joseph was beginning his. Poetry was the new way of life and because of poetry, life for Joseph would never be the same.

Exercise #9- Take everything you've learned and create a master poem.

The End!

ABOUT THE AUTHOR

Chris James is a TEDx speaker, national award-winning poet and revered artist educator who integrates art into education in public schools across America. Through arts education and speaking, Chris inspires people to believe in their inner-power and to express themselves in order to overcome obstacles such as poverty and mental health struggles. He is an author of three books; Black Boy Blues, The Odds Against US and Joe Got Flow(Poetry Hip Hop Children's book). He also wears the hat of Playwright responsible for writing and directing "Dear Black People" and "A Love Like This". Chris is the founder of Arkansas' gallery and poetry venue, The House of Art. As a creative career coach, Chris focuses on helping creative entrepreneurs to make a living off of their craft. As an artist educator, he partners with organizations such as University of Arkansas A+ Schools, THEA Foundation, Arkansas Arts Council, Cultural Arts Council Douglasville, Wildwood Park for the Arts and Arkansas Learning through the Arts. In 2016 Chris launched BUY BACK THE BLOCK, a project where he and partners such as Bank of the Ozarks and other homeowners teach locals how to become homeowners traditionally and nontraditionally. Chris is more than just an artist, he is a visionary and he assures that everyone around him is benefiting.

About The Illustrator

Leron Charles McAdoo, aka Ron Mc, is a visual artist, musician, writer and performer.

In addition to being a lifelong community activist and educator in the LRSD since 1994, he is a member of Phi Beta Sigma Inc. and the co-founder of Backyard Enterprises from 1992. He has participated in numerous programs and events that deal with the issue of race relations and urban needs, some of which include the Healing Racism Institute, Too Cool For School, and the Kuumba Summer Art Academy.

As a Hip Hop advocate and supporter, McAdoo uses the culture of Hip Hop as a vehicle to educate both young and old in the fields of music, writing and art. This can be seen through his annual independently released albums, his many articles for various publications (The Writeous, Fusion, Little Rock Free Press, Arkansas Times, The Dirty Magazine, and TheInkMag.com) his self-published projects entitled, Hip Hop Unheard: Lyrics For The Listening Eye andThe Hip Hoptimist. He is a founding member of the nationally ranked spoken word troupe called Foreign Tongues. Additionally, his portraits, t-shirt designs, murals, comic books and commissioned artwork show his dedication to aesthetics.

Ron Mc has been a radio dj (for 88.3, 98.9, and Power 92.3), co-hosted Art & Literature In Motion TV Show, created and hosted The Mind Blazin' TV Show, engineered for the radio documentary "On The Line: Stories From Ninth Street," produced radio programs (such as The Writeous Hour, Hope From The Hill, and The Skinny), facilitated educational workshops, and volunteered with several organizations such as The Women's Project.

About The Editor

Stacey James McAdoo is a writer, educator and an advocate of literacy. She has participated in several literacy/spoken word organizations such as the SanKofa Poets, Word Up! Poetry Troupe, and Foreign Tongues. In addition she has conducted various writing workshops and poetry readings at local schools, libraries, universities and cultural enrichment programs. Author of Sweet Melanin Messages and Baring My Soul, Stacey James McAdoo is the sponsor of the spoken word youth collective called Writeous Poets and a member of

Alternate Roots (a regional arts service organization that aims to dismantle all forms of oppression).

This sought after arts integration workshop facilitator has also served as the co-producer of the radio documentary, "On the Line: Stories from Ninth Street," copy-editor for The Rock of Arkansas Newspaper, co-host of the television show "Art & Literature in Motion" and co-producer of the youth oriented poetry radio show entitled "The Writeous Hour".

McAdoo holds a B.A. in Professional & Technical Writing, a Master of Arts in Teaching and is a distinguished public school educator. Some of her most recent awards include being named the University of Arkansas' 2017 Distinguished High School Mentor, 2018 Marian G. Lacey/Little Rock School District Educator of the Year and 2019 Regional Arkansas Teacher of the Year. She is currently one of the four finalists in the running for the 2019 Arkansas Teacher of the Year.

Order more copies of *Joe Got Flow* or
schedule Chris James to visit your classroom
by sending an email to
PoetrySavesLivesLR@gmail.com
or Visiting
www.TheChrisJamesJourney.com

51636508R00083

Made in the USA
Columbia, SC
23 February 2019